Frank Walsh

INVESTING&TRADING STRATEGIES:

TIPS AND TOOLS

A clear and intuitive guide to all the tools
and secrets you need to invest profitably

Table of Contents

INTRODUCTION

Trading and investing in stock markets, cryptocurrencies, options, and so on is not as simple as it might seem.

Everyone would love to guess the right stocks, but investing is not a game, nor a lottery. You don't have to guess. Of course, some do, but trying to pick individual stocks on the Stock Exchange based on intuition or, worse, on a stroke of luck, is a highly inefficient way to invest. It may be okay once, but certainly not in the long run.

Investing effectively takes time, complex valuations, and expertise.

In a nutshell, you need the right strategies, tools, and advice from the experts to get the most out of your investments while avoiding the mistakes that almost all beginners make when they start investing.

First of all, therefore, it is good to know the language, terminology, and main concepts of a highly technical world. You need, then, a serious and competent professional to rely on, the so-called broker, who must be the most reliable on the market, not the first one you find. Remember, in fact, that we are talking about your money. Would you trust your money to the first person you see on the street? No, of course not. Looking for a broker is not much different. Take your time, make your evaluations and decide calmly.

On top of that, there are apps. The right ones will make all the difference.

This manual is designed to give you a guide to untangling all these choices.

I'll help you understand how to manage your portfolio, how to find the right broker and the right apps, how to study the market, and I'll share tips and tricks from experienced traders.

Are you ready?

FIVE HUGE MISTAKES
THAT BEGINNERS MAKE

In the event that you can keep away from these slip-ups when you are simply beginning, you will be path in front of the pack and will likewise save yourself a ton of misfortunes and wretchedness.

1. Try not to purchase stocks that are hitting 52-week lows.

We have just examined this point, however it bears rehashing, basically in light of the fact that such countless new brokers lose a ton of cash attempting to get the famous "falling blade." notwithstanding what everybody will advise you, you are quite often much better purchasing a stock that is hitting 52-week highs than one hitting 52-week lows.

Has an organization that you own just announced some truly downright terrible? Assuming this is the case, recollect that there will never be only one cockroach. Awful news comes in bunches.

Numerous investors as of late scholarly this the most difficult way possible with General Electric, which just continued announcing something terrible after another, making the stock slump from 30 to 7. There is nothing of the sort as a "protected stock." Even a blue chip stock can go down a great deal on the off chance that it loses its upper hand or the organization settles on awful choices.

A course of terrible news can regularly make a stock pattern down or hole down more than once. In the event that you own a stock that does this, it is frequently better to get out and stand by a couple of months (or years) to reappear. Again, there will never be only one cockroach.

2. Try not to exchange penny stocks.

A penny stock is any stock that exchanges under $5. Except if you are a high level broker, you ought to stay away from all penny stocks. I would stretch out this by urging you to likewise evade all stocks estimated under $10.

Regardless of whether you have a little exchanging account ($5,000) or less, you are in an ideal situation purchasing less portions of a more expensive stock than a great deal of portions of a penny stock.

That is on the grounds that low-estimated stocks are frequently connected with lower quality organizations. Thus, they are not for the most part permitted to exchange on the NYSE or the Nasdaq. All things considered, they exchange on the OTCBB ("over the counter notice board") or Pink Sheets, the two of which have considerably less rigid monetary announcing prerequisites than the significant trades do.

A considerable lot of these organizations have never made a benefit. They might be fakes or shell organizations that are planned exclusively to improve the board and different insiders. They may likewise incorporate previous "blue chips" that have run into some bad luck like Eastman Kodak or Lehman Brothers.

What's more, penny stocks are characteristically more unstable than more extravagant stocks. Consider it along these lines: if a $100 stock moves $1, that is a 1% move. In the event that a $5 stock moves $1, that is a 20% move. Numerous new brokers belittle the sort of enthusiastic and monetary harm that this sort of instability can cause.

Watcher caution is exhorted.

3. Try not to short stocks.

In the event that you are a high level merchant, don't hesitate to disregard this standard. In the event that you are not, I would truly urge you not to disregard this standard.

To short a stock, you should initially get portions of the stock from your specialist. You at that point sell those offers on the open market. On the off chance that the stock falls in value, you will actually want to repurchase those offers at a lower cost for a benefit.

Assuming, be that as it may, the stock goes up a great deal, you might be compelled to repurchase the offers at a lot greater cost, and wind up losing more cash than you ever had in your exchanging record in any case.

In November 2015, Joe Campbell broke 2 of the 5 precepts. He previously chose to exchange a penny stock called KaloBios Pharmaceuticals. To exacerbate the situation, he chose to short it.

At the point when he hit the sack that night, his exchanging account was worth generally $37,000. At the point when he woke up the following morning, the stock had soar. Thus, not just had he lost the entirety of the $37,000, however he currently owed his intermediary an extra $106,000.

What's more, there was no chance to get out. On the off chance that you owe your dealer cash, they can pull you into court and pursue your home and reserve funds.

Now and then even the most affluent investors can be cleared out by shorting a stock. During the incomparable Northern Pacific Corner of 1901, portions of that railroad stock went from $170 to $1,000 in a solitary day. That move bankrupted the absolute most well off Americans of the day, who had shorted the stock and were then compelled to cover at greater costs.

In the event that you do wind up shorting a stock, recollect that your representative will charge you an expense (normally communicated as a yearly financing cost) to acquire the stock. Also, in the event that you are short a stock, you are liable for delivering any profits on that stock (your specialist will naturally remove the cash from your record quarterly).

For these reasons, shorting stocks is obviously a high level and hazardous exchanging procedure. Try not to attempt it until you've been exchanging for in any event 5 years, and you have the monetary soundness to withstand a stunning upwards move in a stock.

Furthermore, never short a penny stock. It's simply not justified, despite the potential benefits.

4. Try not to exchange on edge.

To short a stock, you should open up an edge account with your

merchant, as Joe Campbell did. You'll likewise require an edge account to exchange stocks utilizing edge.

At the point when you purchase a stock on edge, it implies that you are acquiring cash from your intermediary, to buy a bigger number of portions of stock than you would typically have the option to purchase with simply the money sitting in your investment fund.

Suppose that I have $10,000 in my edge account. Most agents in the U.S.

will permit me to go on edge to buy $20,000 worth of stock in that account. This means they are loaning me an extra $10,000

(for the most part at some over the top yearly loan cost like 11%, which is the thing that E*Trade presently charges) to purchase more portions of stock.

In the event that I purchase $10,000 worth of stock and the stock goes up 10%, I've quite recently made $1,000. However, on the off chance that I can build the measure of stock that I'm purchasing to $20,000

utilizing an edge advance, I will have made $2,000 on a similar 10% move. That will imply that my exchanging account has quite recently gone up by 20% ($2,000/$10,000).

Obviously, if the stock goes down 10% and I'm on full edge, I will have lost 20% of my record esteem. Exchanging on edge is accordingly a type of influence: it enhances the exhibition of your portfolio both on the potential gain and the drawback.

At the point when you purchase a stock utilizing edge, the stock and money in your exchanging account is held as security for the edge advance. On the off chance that the stock falls enough, you might be needed to add more money to your record quickly (this is called

"getting an edge call"), or danger having the specialist drive you to promptly offer your stock to raise money. Frequently this will prompt your selling the stock at the absolute worst time.

At the point when you open up another investment fund and you are given the decision of a "money account" or a "edge account," it's OK to pick "edge account." An edge account has certain favorable circumstances, for example, having the option to utilize the returns from offering a stock to quickly purchase another stock without trusting that the exchange will settle. In the event that you never surpass your money purchasing influence in an edge account, you won't ever be charged expenses or premium. In that manner, it's very conceivable to have an edge account, however never to go on edge.

Assuming, in any case, you don't confide in yourself, open up a "money account." That way, you won't ever be permitted to exchange on edge.

5. Try not to exchange others' thoughts.

The primary explanation never to exchange another person's thoughts is that they presumably don't have the foggiest idea what they are doing. On the off chance that you get a hot stock tip from your neighbor or at the rec center, it's ideal to overlook it. They likely have no clue about the thing they are discussing.

Second, regardless of whether you get a great and genuine exchanging or investing thought from another person, you will presumably not have the conviction to clutch it when difficulties arise. That conviction can just come from building up an exchange thought yourself. At the point when you have planned an exchange, or investigated an investment for yourself, you will have the conviction to hang on. You will likewise know where your stop misfortune is, on the off chance that the stock goes south. Have you seen how hot stock tips never accompanied a suggested stop misfortune level?

Additionally, never place an exchange dependent on something that you have recently perused in Barron's, Forbes, The Wall Street Journal, or have quite recently seen on CNBC. Never purchase a stock dependent on an expert redesign, or sell a stock dependent on an investigator downsize.

I've seen investigators at last minimization a stock just whenever it has fallen half.

Investigators are slacking markers. They will in general overhaul stocks that have just gone up, and downsize stocks that have just dropped down.

There is likewise a solid choice predisposition among experts. The best experts get employed by mutual funds, and you never get with them again. The most exceedingly terrible investigators stay at the banks or business houses, and keep on administering their unremarkable guidance. Gigantic measures of cash have been lost by following their recommendation.

Would it be a good idea for you to try and follow Warren Buffett's recommendation, as I proposed in a past part? Indeed, and no. His recommendation is unquestionably far superior to a hot stock tip from your neighbor. Then again, in the event that you tuned in to him strictly, you passed up the entirety of the incredible tech stocks of the most recent 20 years. He held up until Apple and Amazon were up a huge number of rate focuses before at long last buying them.

Anybody can figure out how to think for themselves in the securities exchange, and concoct their own exchanging and investing thoughts. That is the objective behind the entirety of my books and exchanging courses.

Instead of giving you a fish, I would much rather show you how to look for yourself. That is the way to genuine independence from the rat race.

BUSINESS AND FINANCIAL CONCEPTS

---

1. Net worth

"Your total assets is a proportion of your monetary wellbeing," Storjohann says. It's the consequence of your total assets short the total sum you owe.

You're in acceptable monetary wellbeing if your total assets are all the way into the positives, and you have some work to do if your total assets are anyplace in the negatives. "Total assets can likewise be utilized to quantify how far you've come over the long haul," Storjohann says.

2. Inflation

Swelling alludes to the supported expansion in the cost of products and enterprises. As costs ascend because of swelling, you'll have the option to bear the cost of less and less. Storjohann calls attention to that the authentic expansion rate is 3% each year.

"What's most significant is whether your pay is increasing at a similar rate as expansion," Storjohann says. On the off chance that your compensation isn't staying aware of swelling, you will not have the option to bear the cost of much a couple of years as it were.

3. Liquidity

"Liquidity is the means by which available your cash is," Storjohann says. Money is the most fluid your cash can be, on the grounds that you can get to it right away. While the detachment of specific assets, for example, your home or your retirement accounts, gives them an opportunity to acquire esteem, there are a few situations where you need cash readily available.

"Your backup stash ought to be in a money account since it should be promptly accessible in the event of a crisis," Storjohann says. "Cash you have invested in the stock market isn't as accessible, in light of the fact that you hazard losing some of it on the off chance that you take it out."

4. Bull Market

A buyer market alludes to a market that is on the ascent, which is something to be thankful for. That implies that costs of offers in the market are expanding. Generally, a positively trending market likewise implies the economy is in a decent state, and the degree of joblessness is low. The US is at present in a positively trending market.

5. Bear market

A bear market is something contrary to bull. As such, the market is declining. Offer costs are diminishing, the economy is in a destruction, and joblessness levels are rising.

It seems like something awful (and it absolutely isn't acceptable), however Storjohann says the main thing to remember is that the market is a "rollercoaster," which means it will undoubtedly go here and there and individuals shouldn't freeze each time the market looks somewhat ursine. "Recent college grads have time on their side," she clarifies, "and after some time cash can develop."

6. Risk Tolerance

Recollect that exciting ride we were examining a second prior? As indicated by Storjohann, hazard resistance alludes to how agreeable you are with these swings. "It's about whether you comprehend the cycle or worry about it," she says. How high your danger resistance is determining how forceful you can be with your investments.

Danger resilience isn't simply passionate — it relies upon how long you need to invest, your future acquiring potential, and the assets you have that are not invested, for example, your home or legacy. Significant banks, for example, Wells Fargo, Merrill Lynch, and Vanguard give online apparatuses to help determine your own.

Money managers and Reflection

Your total assets say a ton regarding your monetary circumstance. Flickr/André Benedix

7. Asset allocation and diversification

Asset allotment — where you keep your cash — relies upon your individual requirements and objectives. It's likewise the premise of enhancement.

The objective of expansion is dealing with the danger we addressed in point six — on the off chance that you keep your eggs "across the board bushel," as Storjohann portrays it, what befalls your abundance if the bin falls and breaks? You will need some abundance put away somewhere else. "Expansion considers adjusting," Storjohann says. "You surrender a few potential gains; however, you bring down certain disadvantages."

Know that essentially spreading your investments around probably won't be viable. To be adequately expanded, you must be key about where you invest.

8. Interest

Interest can work possibly in support of you, contingent upon the unique circumstance.

With regards to setting aside cash, "Premium methods your cash will work for you," Storjohann says. At the point when you put your cash in an investment account at a bank, you're allowing that bank to get your cash. Interest is the thing that they pay you to get it; it's a rate that can go up or down contingent upon the condition of the economy.

Then again, when you get cash from somebody — think your charge card backer — you pay revenue to them for acquiring that cash, much the same as the bank paid you to get yours. You'll continue to take care of revenue until you've paid that cash, which is the reason it's essential to avoid obligation, or in case you're paying off debtors, to take care of it as fast as could be expected.

9. Compound interest

Compound interest is revenue that you procure on a "moving equilibrium," and not on the underlying guideline, Storjohann says.

Here's a model: If you get going with $100 acquiring 7% premium yearly, after your first year you'll have $107. The following year, you'll be acquiring 7% premium on $107 and not $100 (you'll procure $7.49 rather than $7).

It doesn't sound so great when we're talking about $7 at a time, but compound interest is the idea that controls the outstanding development of retirement investment funds. As Business Insider's Sam Ro puts it, "It's the deceivingly basic power that makes abundance quickly snowball."

The Power of Compounding Interest

Interest, or simple interest, is an aggregate you pay for having utilized a monetary assistance, for example, the interest you pay to the bank for a home loan or any loan specified.

As you most likely are aware, the longer the span of the loan, the more prominent the generally

interest you pay to the bank, in light of the fact that the last will take more time to gather the whole sum that has been progressed to you.

We should make a qualification quickly: simple or compound interest?

Simple interest is the one characterized above, while compound interest will be interest on interest.

We contextualize simple interest and compound interest both in the realm of monetary investments, which is the thing that interests us explicitly.

Simple interest is the return that is paid to you reliably, in light of an underlying invested capital, which doesn't increment since you intermittently pull out the profit.

I'll give you a solid model.

Invest an amount of $20,000 in an instrument with which you procure 10% per annum, you will get yourself an amount of $22,000 toward the year's end; in this way pull out the $2,000 of benefit and rehash a similar investment with the underlying capital consistently of $20,000.

Following 10 years you will get yourself $40,000, or you will have multiplied the underlying capital.

Compound interest, then again, depends on the ceaseless reinvestment of the collected profit, without the withdrawal toward the year's end.

Take a similar model again yet, in the wake of procuring $2,000 in the principal year, invest the total amassed capital in the subsequent year, for example the amount of $22,000 and not $20,000 as in the primary model.

The underlying invested capital will step by step increment after every year and subsequently the yearly profit will increment appropriately.

In this subsequent case, following 10 years you will procure $51,875.

In the picture underneath you can perceive what occurs in the two instances of simple interest and compound interest.

Initial Investment	$20.000
Annual interest rate	10,00%
Investment duration (years)	10

Future value with simple interest: 20.000+(20.000*10%)*10 =	$40.000
Future value with compound interest without P.A.C.: VF=20.000*(1+10/1)^10 =	$51.875
Simple net interest	$20.000
Net compound interest without P.A.C.	$31.875

	Int. Simple	nt. Compound without PAC
Total capital	$40.000	$51.875
Interest only	$20.000	$31.875

Do you comprehend the significance of compound interest and for what reason do you need to utilize it to acquire over the long run?

Disregard simple interest and from this point forward stress over taking advantage of compound interest in your investments.

The power of compounding interest is one of the most useful financial tools at one's disposal. First and foremost, it stresses the importance of saving money from early on to maximize the total amount obtained later in life. Secondly, it uses compound interest to reach the ambitious goal of amassing $500,000.00 by the time one's life is over. Thirdly, it emphasizes that not only does one need a lot of money saved up but also must follow the advised system of putting aside money without interruption. If one quits saving after just five years then they will have accumulated less than $100,000.00! The power of compounding interest is powerful but not every investment plan can survive in its wake. It is important to avoid risky investments and to stick with those that are more stable like bonds and savings accounts that traditionally have higher interest rates than other types of investments.

"With these facts in mind, it will not be hard for you to understand how the ordinary person can become wealthy. It is not a question of miracle or luck. It is a matter of knowledge-knowledge and application."

How Market Works

The first question you probably have is what causes these fluctuations in the first place. The answer is a little more complex than most people think. It's true that there are many factors that can cause market changes, but they're a response to changes in consumer demand, which is actually caused by inflation and unemployment rates. Yes, it's about supply and demand; we all know about this concept, right? Rest assured, these concepts aren't just complicated for complicatedness' sake! Instead, they help you understand how market movements occur and how you can use them to your advantage when trading or investing.

When you go out and purchase something, you're creating demand. You put money into the economy, and that money goes into someone else's pocket. That person then uses it to buy a candy bar or a new pair of shoes, and then he or she might spend that money on beer or cigarettes. This endless cycle eventually creates inflation. What does this have to do with markets? Well, when you see market shifts, they're usually triggered by changes in inflation or unemployment rates. Investors will sell their stocks or bonds if they are worried that inflation is going to rise and may make those investments worthless.

Unemployment and inflation rates are caused by various factors, such as technological advances or the global economy, which means that you can't predict them from looking at the news. However, one thing is certain: if these rates change drastically in a short period of time, investors will sell their stocks because of the possibility of more inflation. You might be wondering how a change in unemployment rates would create a change in market behavior, but this is actually very straightforward if you understand how governments usually deal with these problems. When an economy suffers from high levels of unemployment, the government will often engage in expansionary fiscal policy, which means they are borrowing money to stimulate spending. As a result of borrowing money, interest rates will fall because there's more cash chasing after bonds; this can stimulate more spending and economic activity. In response to this, inflation will rise a bit. Once the economy is stimulated, investors feel more comfortable investing their money in those companies that are doing well.

PERSONAL ADVISOR AND ONLINE BROKERS

Your financial security is important. However, for some of us, it can be an area we find difficult to understand and manage. That's why so many of us turn to an advisor – someone who has experience in these areas and can help you make decisions that will keep your finances on the right track. So what are your options?

A personal advisor is a good option for people who would like one-on-one guidance with their finances. They will typically take a holistic approach, looking at all aspects of your financial life from debt to taxes to savings. Personal advisors might charge by the hour or they might have a set monthly fee, depending on their arrangement with you. Benefits: A personal advisor will look at your whole financial picture and help you make decisions that are right for your life situation. You'll have one primary point person who is available to you and to whom you can build a relationship. Potential drawbacks: Personal advisors are often expensive, though they might be willing to offer a free consultation in order to win your business.

An online broker is an automated way to invest that comes with the expertise and industry contacts of an independent investment firm. The internet-based platforms for these types of accounts are easy to use, but they also offer personalized advice from expert analysts who can help you choose the investments that best fit your goals. Benefits: Online brokers can be a good option for people who are comfortable doing their own financial research but want help from people with experience. These types of advisors can allow you to invest on your own, but also give you the benefit of a team behind the scenes that can offer advice and answer questions. Potential drawbacks: If you are nervous about investing without seeing what you are buying, this isn't for you. There is no ability to ask the analyst for advice; an online platform makes recommendations based on your goals and risk tolerance.

Every day, consumers are bombarded with messages from online brokers and advisors. With so many different solutions to choose from, it's hard for people to know which one is best. Additionally, the products they offer are typically not easy to compare because there are no universal standards in the financial industry. This makes selecting an advisor and broker very challenging for people who are new to investing or don't have time to research all the options themselves.

We've gone through it too, and have put together some helpful tips that make the comparison easier. If you're planning to use any of the services listed in this report, you should pay attention to the following factors:

1) **Education.**

The first and most important thing to check is educational background. Does it have any? What are they? These degrees will tell you what kind of investor the advisor is. For example, if it has a finance-related degree, such as MSc in Financial Analysis or Certified Financial Planner, then it can give you an idea whether it will be able to provide intelligent and relevant advice. For people who want a more personal touch in their lives, such as with health or relationship issues, a Master's degree in psychology or social work may be best for them.

2)Experience.

The second most important factor is how long has the advisor been in business. You want someone who has been established and remained relevant for at least a few years, because this shows it has survived and grown based on the quality of service it provides.

3)Licenses and Insurance.

Brokers can be certified by organizations such as Chartered Financial Analyst (CFA), Certified Financial Planner (CFP), Chartered Life Underwriter (CLU), Chartered Life Specialist (CLS) or Registered Investment Advisor (RIA). They ensure that a professional follows certain ethical standards and maintain a proper level of education required to serve you better.

Most of the time, these credentials mean the advisor is an experienced professional in the industry. But it doesn't mean they are a good fit for you. They're just a sign that you can trust what they offer because these licenses have qualifications that can only be gained through meaningful coursework and relevant experience.

It is also important to double check that your advisors carry liability insurance and fidelity bond, which protect you if something goes wrong. The reason you need to be cautious about this is because there are some dishonest individuals in the financial world who may wish to take advantage of unwary customers. The best way to avoid this is to only deal with well-established and reputable brokers.

4)Tax Filing Services.

Many people do not consider the importance of picking a qualified tax filing service, which is only natural because most of us do not like dealing with numbers, especially when it comes to taxes. But tax filing services are important because they can help make sure you stay on top of your taxes and also ensure that you're not audited by the government for paying too little or too much in taxes. This will save a lot of headaches for you over the years, as running afoul with the IRS can result in a painful consequence if you fail to pay them properly or handle your expenses incorrectly.

5)Investment Portfolio.

Some brokers are solely online investment platforms and do not offer any other services. On the other hand, some of them manage funds and stocks directly for you as a customer. This requires special licensing and also brings with its certain risks, so you want to make sure you choose a solution that is most appropriate for your unique needs.

6)Commissions and Fees.

While the commissions may vary from one broker to another, the main thing you need to look at is whether or not they charge fees on top of their commissions. This can be quite costly over time because it can add up exponentially if you do not check or evaluate your portfolio often enough. This is why it's better to go with a broker that only charges commissions, which will not cost you anything else.

7)Brokerage Accounts and Products.

As for the products they offer, many brokers have low or no-minimum requirements, which is great because it ensures more people can get into the market without having to make a large upfront investment.

8)Customer Service.

Lastly, do they have good customer service? All companies offer some form of customer support these days, but some of these are just unaccountably bad – so much so that it seems like they do not care about their clients at all. This is why you should really make sure the company you're dealing with has good customer service, which should be both prompt and thorough.

A good broker will not just find you the right financial products to invest in, but will also help you monitor your investment portfolio as well as provide education every step of the way. This will ensure that your investments grow steadily and without any undue risk. The end goal is to have a steady stream of passive income for retirement that allows you to comfortably live out the last years of your life in peace and happiness.

How to Open a Broker Account?

Opening a broker account is incredibly simple; all you need to provide is basic information (name, address, social security number) and then deposit money into the account so that you are able to start trading with real money on the market.

For example, we'll use our Fundraise page where you can invest in commercial real estate and REITs (that's a quick summary of what those are). If you click on the "Open account" button, you'll need to fill out the page that pops up.

When we click the "buy real estate with as little as $500" button, we get a form like this that appears:

You will need to click "continue" at the bottom of the blue bar that says "Personal information." Then provide your name and address in the fields provided.

You'll need to provide your social security number (or your tax id) and agree to the terms of service when you click the "Fill out my account application" button.

After filling that out, you'll be brought to a page that asks for your financial account information:

Make sure you only put in information for whatever bank or brokerage account you want to deposit money into! If you haven't done so yet, we recommend signing up for a brokerage account with one of our partners by clicking here. Let them know you found them on Fundrise! After completing this form, check your email again as we should have a message from our partner there waiting for us.

Finally, you'll get to this page where you will be able to deposit money into your brokerage account. I recommend depositing $500 or more but at least $100 so that you are able to start trading on the market. This is an easy way for us introduce you to investing with Fundrise and what it's like. You can read through the rest of our website to learn more about it if you want! In fact, in a few minutes we'll explore how much money is required as well as how much profit has been made using our service.

BEST INVESTING AND MICRO SAVINGS APPS

The world is changing. People are working more and more hours on two jobs. There is less time to do things that you enjoy and too much work to do in your spare time. Many people have no choice but to work hard for the money, but there's still a choice about how you invest that money, which can make all the difference in your future financial health.

Investing Vs Micro Savings Apps

We have been taught that the stock market is how you make money. However, it has become increasingly difficult to access stock market investments and sometimes even to understand them. The methods that used to work aren't as reliable as they used to be, and investing in individual stocks can be risky.

The other alternative is micro savings apps – which in our opinion are less work, more convenient and more secure than stock trading / investing. They also have the potential for being much more profitable in the long-term because of their compound interest rate multipliers built in. This means your money really grows on itself and the more it makes, the more it can make. This is as opposed to stock market investments in which you must wait for a company to pay out dividends (if they do) or sell your stock at a profit.

In addition, micro savings apps can be used and accessed from anywhere in the world with an internet connection, so you can invest your money from anywhere without having to deal with geographical restrictions.

The Best Micro Savings Apps

We have chosen these apps by considering budget, time available to make money, acquired financial experience and of course their potential return on investment.

1. Acorns

With Acorns, you can invest your money as frequently as you want and have it automatically withdrawn from your debit card or bank account.

The Acorns "Roundup" feature allows customers to make micro savings for free each time they shop at a retailer with a supported credit or debit card, without changing their shopping habits. Whenever a purchase is made, the app rounds up to the nearest dollar and invests the remaining change into an Acorns portfolio.

Acorns has also partnered with influential business leaders such as Yahoo CEO Marissa Mayer and Uber board member Bill Gurley to offer challenges that can earn its users additional cash rewards for investing early, often, and responsibly.

Additionally, the app has an easy-to-understand and user-friendly interface that makes it accessible to new investors.

The only drawback is fees – Acorns charges $1 a month for balances under $5,000 (or 0.25 percent of assets per year); $2 a month for balances above that threshold (or 0.25

percent). You can also try out Acorns' free version for 14 days.

2. Stash

Stash's goal is to make investing simple and cost effective. The app serves as a platform for every type of investment from trading stocks, to spending your spare change. Unlike other apps on the market, Stash offers customers the ability to choose how they want to invest their money- by selecting an area of personal interest like "politics" or "sports".

If you're not sure where to start, the app will also suggest a portfolio based on your age and financial goals.

Initially launched in 2015, Stash has gone through several iterations in terms of features and functionality with its newest release in March 2017.

The current version of the app allows users to:

Invest as little as $5 at a time across hundreds of different investments (no minimum balance requirement).

Decide how they wish to be billed (quarterly, monthly, yearly).

Link up a bank account or debit card for easy and convenient automated investing.

Choose from hundreds of stocks, bonds, ETFs, and cryptocurrencies.

Recent updates to the app include "Watch lists" – which allow users to track relevant stocks and cryptocurrencies in real time. For those who want more information about the principles behind investing their money, "Stash University" is an interactive investing course that walks users through key concepts like diversification and risk tolerance.

3. Acorns Spend

Acorns recently launched Acorns Spend, a free app that is similar to the original app, but instead of investing your money, you can save it with it.

Though the two apps have similarities – like round up and invest features and checklists – they differ in the fact that

Acorns Spend allows customers to spend their spare change without having to make adjustments to their financial habits.

With a linked debit or credit card, Acorns Spend round up your purchases like Acorns and invests the change using the same investment portfolio found in its other app, while also eating into your debit or credit card's budget.

What sets this app apart from the competition is its generous savings potential – users can save up to 5.4 percent, or $1,215 a year for someone making $50,000 annually- based on the app's tax efficiency algorithm. The algorithm works by identifying financial opportunities and effectively minimizing your tax obligations by maximizing your pre-tax dollars.

Another feature that sets Acorns Spend apart from other apps of its kind is the fact that it allows customers to spend their money in real time without any account minimums or monthly fees for balances under $5,000 (or 0.25 percent of assets per year).

However, if users are looking to invest their savings instead of spend them, they will have to upgrade to the regular Acorns or Acorns Later app.

4. M1 Finance

Founded in 2014 by Alex Friedman and Jacob Gibson, M1 Finance is a free mobile app that allows customers to manage and invest their money. Similar to Robinhood, M1 offers commission-free trading on thousands of ETFs and stocks with no minimum account balance required.

The app's tax optimization feature helps customers maximize the after-tax growth potential of their investments by identifying cost basis opportunities (read more details here).

Even though it is free to use, M1 charges a fee of $0.0035 for every stock trade and an ETF trading fee of $0.0025 for every share traded.

M1 also offers a "Smart Deposit" feature that automatically invests the money users deposit into their M1 account into their respective investment portfolios. The more money customers deposit into their accounts, the more money they will have in their investment portfolios (up to $15,000).

The company offers taxable users two custodial accounts: one with short-term capital gains and one with long-term capital gains.

One drawback for M1 is that users have to manually invest their money, which is an annoyance for those who don't have a solid understanding of investments and trading. Another drawback is that there isn't a mobile-based app to manage accounts from iOS devices. However, M1 does have an iPhone app, but it doesn't look as polished as Robinhood's.

Currently, only Savers can sign up for an account; but soon Investors will be able to sign up too.

5. Tiller

Tiller provides a service called "Bill Paying Made Simple. " According to the company's website:

"Tiller is a smart, easy to use personal finance manager that gives you the tools to better understand and manage your money. With Tiller, you can quickly see where your money is going and take control without spending tons of time analyzing spreadsheets or inputting data."

Here's how it works: Customers pay certain bills from their checking accounts (i.e. rent, credit cards bill, car loans, etc.) through their Tiller account for free with no fees.

There are different tiers of service offered by Tiller depending on what you pay them each month.

For example, the most basic level of service costs $2.50 per month for customers who pay an average of $500 per month in bills through the service.

The second tier costs $4.95 a month for customers with monthly payments totaling more than $1,000. The third level charges 5.95 monthly for those who pay more than $5,000 in bills a month through the service.

Using Tiller to Pay Bills Can Save You Money

It might not seem like paying a few bucks to save yourself hours of work is worth it but when you consider all the time you'll save over your lifetime on tedious tasks, it is well worth it.

The company is also taking longer to achieve profit-making status. In 1998 and 1999, 89 percent of the companies funded by venture capitalists went public or were acquired within 4 years. This year, the figure was 64 percent.

"Roughly half the venture-backed companies we are interested in are going to be acquired before they go public," says Donald E. Boyd, founder of Venture Economics, a consulting firm in Menlo Park, Calif., who has been tracking private stock markets since 1996.

The shift from initial public offerings to mergers may reflect an increase in Internet companies that are not yet profitable but have strong brand names and sites with loyal users.

The company grew quickly and in March 2000, less than a year after going public, Amazon agreed to be acquired by online bookseller Barnes & Noble for $1.45 billion.

"We're in the second wave of venture-capital investing," says Michael Sinkin, who runs Red Mile Group Inc., an e-commerce consulting firm in New York. "It's much more likely now that venture capitalists will make money through an acquisition. It's harder to make money through an IPO."

The second wave may last longer, too. "In the 1990s," says Mr. Sinkin, "I'd see venture capitalists get excited about a new idea and try it out. If it didn't work, they'd fold up and move on to something else." Now that e-commerce and e-business are mature industries, people expect to spend years working on them. There is little doubt that the venture capitalists will be along for the ride.

In the meantime, they are making money from companies like Tiller. The company charges a monthly fee of $2.50 to $5.95 for its services, but the savings can far outweigh the costs. For example, instead of letting your landlord collect your rent on a monthly basis by sending you a check or charging it to your credit card, you can have all of your rent automatically withdrawn from your checking account and sent directly to him or her—and save yourself the transaction fee and the time spent writing out checks.

Here's how it works: You can use Tiller to pay all federal bills that charge a flat fee plus postage (such as income tax payments). You can also ask any company that sends invoices to you (such as your cable-TV provider) whether it will accept payments through Tiller. Once you have set up a biller on Tiller, you can pay your bills right through your bank account.

6. Robinhood Financial (Formerly "Robinhood")

The Robinhood app, which lets users trade U.S. stocks for free, provides an easy-to-use platform that can help anyone learn the basics of investing in the stock market and save money on commissions.

The app is fairly intuitive – users can tap on a company's name to see how it's performing or tap on the menu icon to view all available stocks and options and their respective prices in real time (unlike other apps that only provide stock information).

INSIDER'S SECRET OF
THE STOCK MARKET

Allow me to begin by helping you to remember quite possibly the main realities about the stock market:

Response to the news is in every case more significant than the actual news.

Thus, likewise:

Response to an income report is in every case more significant than the profit report itself.

It's quite often a bearish sign when a stock auctions after a decent income report. On the off chance that a stock that has had a major run-up falls on a decent profit report, it very well might be an indication that the upturn is finished.

The inverse is likewise obvious. At the point when a stock actually revitalizes after a "awful" profit report, it is a bullish sign. It's additionally a bullish sign if the stock market rallies after a negative financial report.

Numerous individuals get difficult and attempt to guide the stock market. Savvy dealers tune in to the market all things being equal.

Because you need to bring in cash today doesn't imply that the chance will be naturally accessible. You should figure out how to be content with what the market is at present ready to offer you.

Try not to drive an exchange. Be patient, and sit tight for the fat pitch. On the off chance that you can learn persistence and order, the market will at last reward you beyond anything you could ever imagine.

Zero in on a couple of stocks, and become more acquainted with how they exchange. Try not to extended yourself excessively far by attempting to follow such a large number of stocks.

On the off chance that you have committed an error, cut your misfortunes rapidly and proceed onward. Never let an exchange transform into a drawn out investment. Try not to average exchanging misfortunes. Try not to squander valuable resources. Never add to a losing position, however don't hesitate to add to a position once it begins to bring in cash.

The stock market is a limiting machine. That implies that it takes all accessible data about an organization and the economy and changes a stock's cost in like manner. In some cases, it makes a preferable showing of this over different occasions. The stock market tends to over-markdown recognized dangers, and under-rebate unidentified dangers.

At whatever point you continue to find out about a danger in the monetary news, it is in all likelihood previously valued into a stock, or the stock market all in all. The dangers you are not hearing anything about, or that appear to be ludicrously far-fetched, that can cause the most harm. In the event that everybody is looking at something, it's quite often as of now estimated into the market. That implies that the stock has just moved to where it should be, founded on the entirety of the data that is as of now accessible. To bring in cash in exchanging or investing, you need to skate to where the puck will be, not to where it has just been.

A market that consistently neglects to move higher will typically go down. The stock market (just as individual stocks) will consistently look out our weaknesses, and move so as to make the most extreme agony the greatest number of merchants.

Temporarily, mass brain science manages the markets, not essentials or the economy. Improving organization essentials and great monetary news will frequently appear in stock costs before they appear in the features, which is the reason it is so imperative to follow through on regard for cost activity.

However long the market is going up, and your stock is going up, don't be in a rush to take benefits. To dominate at this match, you should have a few

huge victors. Try not to interfere with them too early.

There is an irregularity to the stock market that we ought not disregard.

Albeit the 2 most well-known stock market declines both happened in October (1929 and 1987), September has generally been the most fragile month for the stock market.

Normal recorded returns for June and August are additionally negative.

This has prompted the renowned articulation "Sell in May and disappear." Stock market gets back from November through April have verifiably been a lot higher than stock market gets back from May through October. This doesn't really imply that you should offer the entirety of your stocks and go to money each May. However, it implies that you ought to be more careful when exchanging throughout the mid-year months. Numerous merchants and investors are at the sea shore, so liquidity is lower and instability is higher.

On the off chance that you are searching for a decent long haul investment, purchase an organization that has the most elevated deals in its industry. So for home improvement, you need to possess Home Depot; for inexpensive food, McDonald's; for toothpaste, Colgate Palmolive; for installments, Visa; for PDAs, Apple; and for online media, Facebook.

When a business sells more than some other organization in its industry, it turns out to be hard to rival. There's not a viable replacement for being #1 in your industry.

At the point when the entirety of the specialists concurs, at that point something other than what's expected will occur in the market. The current customary way of thinking is in every case previously evaluated into the market.

Here are a portion of my record-breaking most loved statements about exchanging and the stock market.

George Soros: "It's not whether you're correct or wrong that is significant, but rather how much cash you make when you're correct and the amount you lose when you're off-base."

John Maynard Keynes: "Markets can stay nonsensical longer than you can stay dissolvable."

Dennis Gartman: "The markets will get back to soundness the second that you have been delivered bankrupt."

William Eckhardt: "Either an exchange is sufficient to take, in which case it ought to be actualized at full size, or it's not worth wasting time with by any means."

Ed Seykota: "Basics that you read about are ordinarily pointless as the market has just limited the cost, and I call them 'clever mentals.' I am basically a pattern merchant with bits of hunches dependent on around twenty years of involvement. Arranged by significance to me are: (1) the drawn out pattern, (2) the current diagram example, and (3) picking a decent spot to purchase or sell. Those are the three essential segments of my exchanging. Path down in far off fourth spot are my crucial thoughts and, very likely, on equilibrium, they have cost me cash."

Jim Rogers: "I simply stand by until there is cash lying in the corner, and i should simply go over yonder and get it. I don't do anything meanwhile. Indeed, even individuals who lose cash in the market say, 'I just lost my cash, presently I need to plan something for make it back.' No, you don't. You ought to stay there until you discover something."

Bruce Kovner: "At whatever point I enter a position; I have a foreordained stop.

That is the lone way I can rest. I realize where I'm getting out before I get in.

The position size on an exchange is dictated by the stop, and the stop is resolved on a specialized premise."

Paul Tudor Jones: "Don't be a saint. Try not to have a sense of self. Continuously question yourself and your capacity. Never feel that you are excellent. The subsequent you do, you are dead. My greatest hits have consistently come after I have had an incredible period and I began to believe that I knew something."

Ed Seykota: "The way to long haul endurance and thriving has a great deal to do with the cash the executives strategies consolidated into the specialized framework. There are old brokers and there are striking dealers, however there are not many old, intense merchants."

Bulls bring in cash, bears bring in cash, however pigs get butchered. An avaricious merchant who disregards his stop

misfortunes and other leave signs will offer back the
entirety of his benefits, to say the very least.

SOME OF THE TOP TRADERS IN THE STOCK MARKET

With regards to offering monetary guidance, barely any individuals can enthrall a group of people very like Warren Buffet can. His uncommon achievement in the realm of investments - also his $85 billion fortune - implies even those not a tiny smidgen inspired by money sit up and listen when Buffett shares his top tips for accumulating riches.

However, Buffett is something beyond the amount of his bank balance (a ten-figure number to be careful). His life is covered in an energy for business and investments and, notwithstanding his tremendous riches, he is broadly known for his liberality and thriftiness - he actually lives in the very home in Omaha in Nebraska that he purchased for $31,000 in 1958 and all the more as of late he has vowed to part with 99% of his abundance to noble cause.

His story is a captivating one without a doubt. Who is Warren Buffet? What are a portion of his rules that you can apply in your life and business? What would you be able to gain from Buffett's own encounters about dealing with your life, cash and vocation?

Buffett has just stood up to and beaten life's difficulties and made a way that could fill in as a triumphant guide for you. You should simply follow that way on your approach to progress. You'll have to change and modify it a little to meet your own circumstances and conditions, however the outline is to a great extent set up. Throughout everyday life and business, you can benefit as much as possible from the intelligence learned by effective and affluent individuals who've made an imprint for themselves around the world and use it as a manual for accomplish your own objectives.

For quite a long time, Buffett has been a good example to thousands, if not millions, of growing business visionaries and individuals quick to have an effect in their lives.

His prosperity has affected the activities of finance managers all around the planet and has filled in as an uncommon norm to take a stab at both expertly and by and by, gratitude to his liberality and eagerness to help other people. His impact spreads all over and even those among the most extravagant on the planet have received Buffett's life draws near. Because of

Buffett's consolation, for instance, in excess of 160 very rich people have consented to give and part with at any rate half of their abundance for humanitarian causes.

Paul Tudor Jones

Paul Tudor Jones is an American Investor, a mutual funds administrator and he is otherwise called a humanitarian. Jones was brought into the world on September 28th, 1954. His adoration for Hedge store the board drove him to open his firm back in 1980, an organization by the name Tudor Investment Corporation. The organization's central command was being as yet situated in Greenwich, associate cut, and it had some expertise in the administration of resources. Later on, he made Tudor gathering which is a speculative stock investments Holding Company. The

Tudor fence organization worked in the administration of fixed pay, monetary standards, values and furthermore products.

Throughout the most recent years, his organizations have been doing extraordinary procuring him incredible fortunes since in February 2017, he was assessed to have a net of 4.7 billion by Forbes magazine and this caused him to be number 120 the of the richest individuals on the planet on the class of 400 individuals positioned on the magazine.

Tim Cook

Timothy Donald Cook is the American leader, Industrial Engineer, and Developer. He is at present the Chief boss at the workplaces of Apple Inc. This is the new position he gained at the Apple Inc. since he recently functioned as the Chief Operating Officer under the originator Steve Jobs. Joined Apple in the year 1998 as the senior VP of overall tasks and afterward he later filled in as the chief VP of the world in the division of deals and administrations. In 24th March 2011, he was elevated to turn into the Chief leader.

He is associated with his dynamic advocation of different mankind and natural development which incorporate the transformation of political of global and nearby observation, online protection, enterprise tax assessment both broadly and universally. Conditions conservation and furthermore the American assembling act.

In the year 2014, Cook became public and recognized himself as a gay and was recorded among the 500 CEO at Fortune magazine. Different organizations that Cook worked at incorporate; he was an individual from the leading group of sheets of heads of Nike-inc., the public football establishment, the trustee of Duke University.

Around 2012, the Apple Inc organization chose to give Cook a pay

of offers worth huge number of dollars vesting in 2016 to 2021. During a public discourse; Cook said that his income from the allowed stocks would be offered to good cause establishments. This incorporates all that he possesses.

George Soros

George Soros was brought into the world in Budapest, Hungary on August 12, 1930 as György Schwartz. He was destined to Tivadar and Erzsébet Schwartz. The family was of Jewish plunge yet decided to not practice their religion because of the way that enemy of Semitism was on the ascent in Hungary. As an upper-working class family, they didn't wish to have their family to be under suspect and investigated. To keep away from this, they changed their last name to Soros, which signifies "assigned replacement" in Hungarian. This name was preferred by Soros' dad for its importance as well as on the grounds that it was spelled the equivalent forward as it is in reverse.

After this name change, Nazi Germany came to involve Hungary in March of 1944. The Nazi's set up a Jewish Council, Judunrat in which all Jewish youngsters needed to report. They were not, at this point permitted to went to their normal schools. This committee was responsible for expelling any Jews that were found in Hungary. They picked school-matured youngsters to be the ones to bring the extradition notification to individuals.

As of now, Soros was 13 years of age and had gotten papers himself to provide for Jewish attorneys. His dad, Tivadar, encouraged him to caution individuals as he gave them out that on the off chance that they appeared at work that they would be expelled.

During this unstable time, deception should have been made to ensure large numbers of the Jewish public. Soros' folks shrouded their Jewish roots once more by buying reports that expressed their "Christian" confidence. This assisted them with enduring the Nazi occupation. Youthful George even needed to profess to be the "godson" to an authority of the Hungarian government for his own assurance.

George was placed in a circumstance where he needed to go with this authority to a Jewish family's domain to take stock. He was not a piece of the interaction himself, but rather needed to observe the occasion. The authority who was securing Soros had his nearby association with the Jewish individuals since his significant other was Jewish too. She had just sought refuge now.

Through endeavors like these, numerous Jewish individuals were ensured in Hungary.

The endeavors of Soros' dad to help individuals during this time set in youthful Soros' psyche that his dad was an extraordinary legend and a defender to the Jewish public.

At long last, an end went to the stowing away in 1945 when the Nazi's left their control of Hungary. Soros had the option to leave Hungary not long after the Nazi retreated in the time of 1947. Presently he could seek after an instruction in London. He emigrated to England where he went to the London School of Economics as an understudy of Carl Popper, a savant. In 1951, he got his Bachelor of Science in Philosophy. He finished school in 1954 with a Master of Science in way of thinking.

Carl Icahn

Carl Icahn was brought into the world on Feb 16, 1936, and he is a notable money manager in America. Aside from possessing a few organizations, he was likewise and still most popular for being a sensible investor and givers as well. He established the Icahn Enterprises, and he is the regulator of all the organization's offer since he is the biggest investor. The organization is huge, and it is situated in the New York City. Of late the organization is known as the combination Holding organization, however at first, it was alluded to as American Real Bequest Partners. Cahn has additionally led in the Federal-Mogul organization which works in creating fabricating and furthermore providing the powertrain parts and vehicle security items.

Carl has additionally won hearts of numerous because of his business strategies whereby he was named as the corporate bandit because of his capacity to benefit from the threatening takeover and the resource depriving of the American aircraft. Forbes magazine took a gander at his abundance, and he is assessed to have a sum of 16.6 billion dollars by 2017. He was additionally positioned as number 26 of the most well off individuals in work on the 400 rich individual's classes. In the support business world, Carl has all the earmarks of being on top five of most well off men taking the last position.

HOW TO MANAGE YOUR INVESTMENT PORTFOLIO?

If you're retired and have been accumulating investments over the years, don't you think it's about time to start managing them?

You may be wondering what the best way is to manage your investments. Should you invest in stocks, bonds, annuities or other securities?

There are a lot of options out there and it can get overwhelming quickly.

What are some things I should think about when managing my portfolio?

The method of diversification is probably one of the most important aspects in an investment plan. Diversification will help you reap the benefits of investing in a number of different areas and decrease your risk.

You want to choose investments that will perform differently during different market conditions.

For example, if you are expecting inflation, then stocks that produce more income will be beneficial during an inflationary period. If you're planning on retiring in 10 years, then growth investments would be better at this time.

If you only have one type of investment in your portfolio (such as all bonds or all stocks), then it could severely hurt your performance if there is a downturn in that market. If there was an economic downturn and interest rates fell, being too heavily invested in bonds could cause real problems for your portfolio.

What are the types of securities to consider when managing my portfolio?

There are different types of securities you can invest in. Some include:

Stocks – These are shares of the ownership (or equity) in a company. When you purchase a stock, you own a small piece of that company and hopefully the value will rise over time.

Bonds – Shares in a company's debt or loans made to that organization. Bond prices also go up and down as interest rates change. They pay interest on the loan at regular intervals, usually annually or semi-annually.

Mutual Funds – An investment fund offered by a company or bank that owns a number of different investments. The fund shareholders own various parts of different companies' stocks, bonds, or other securities.

Annuities – A contract that pays the owner a specific amount at predetermined times over time. This can be a good way to save for college or retirement.

What are the types of accounts in which I can invest?

When managing your portfolio, you want to look into all of your options for investing. There are three main accounts:

Individual Retirement Accounts (IRA), Roth IRA and Traditional IRA.

The main difference between these accounts is how they are taxed and what happens at retirement age with each account.

With a Traditional IRA, you pay taxes on the money now, but when you retire, the taxes will be taken out of your withdrawals. Therefore, there is the greatest potential for growth in this account.

With a Roth IRA, after more than five years with the account (or turning age 59 ½) you can withdraw your contributions at any time and for any reason without being taxed on them. You'll still have to pay taxes on the growth in value though.

With an IRA, the money can be withdrawn without penalty at retirement age, but there are early withdrawal penalties if withdrawn before that.

Where should I open my account?

The type of account you have is up to you. But, there are different types of investment accounts. When deciding where to open an account, consider:

If you're going to be managing your portfolio yourself, opening your account at an online brokerage is probably the best route. You will have access to thousands of funds and other securities that can be traded fairly easily.

Also consider opening accounts at multiple institutions so that you can diversify and have more control over your assets.

You want to choose a firm that has low fees for trading and managing your portfolio.

What should I track when managing my portfolio?

There are a number of different statistics that will be useful to you when managing your portfolio:

Dividend Paying Stocks – They are stocks that pay dividends and the distribution will be recorded in a separate section of your account. This means you are getting a portion of the company's profits, which is a great thing for long term growth.

Dividend Yield – This is the annual dividend rate expressed as a percentage. For example, if a stock pays $1.00 per year and it sells for $10.00, then it has an annual dividend yield of 10%.

Market Price – The current price of the security and it will fluctuate over time.

Shares Outstanding – This tells you how many other investors own a piece of the company as well. If there are a lot of shares outstanding, then the stock price has to rise a bit more to get the same return on your investment.

Shares in Float – This is the number of shares that are available for trading and are not owned by private investors or insiders. More shares in float means there is more liquidity on the market. However, this can also mean that there's greater chance of fraud because those "floating" shares don't have a registered owner that can be found doing basic research work.

If you are looking for investment information on a specific company, check the "Insiders" tab in the security detail page on Yahoo Finance. This will give you information about the holdings of management and how many shares are held by them. This can be useful to find out if there is insider trading going on or if they have large holdings that might be causing them to have inside information.

What are some tips and tricks I should know?

There are a number of different tips and tricks that will help you maximize your returns when managing your portfolio:

Diversification – Diversifying over multiple industries, market cap sizes, company size and other factors can reduce risk and make it easier for you to achieve your goals.

Tax Loss Harvesting – If you have a taxable account and the price of a particular stock dips, sell it before the end of the year to minimize your tax burden, assuming your overall portfolio will be taxed at a lower rate than during the stock's high.

Deferring Capital Gains Taxes – You can avoid paying capital gains taxes by not selling until after your first year anniversary with the investment.

Don't Panic – You should invest in companies that you understand and research hard so that you can make a calculated decision with real information. If something happens that would cause you to lose sleep at night or decide your life priorities have changed, then sell it.

There's no need to sell a stock because of a few bad quarters. Analyze the company and see if it has any long term issues that would make you unable to sleep at night.

How do I properly rebalance my portfolio?

Rebalancing means taking profits from stocks or sectors that have done well and reinvesting that money in other areas. For example, if you had a portfolio with $1000 worth of stocks in the technology sector and their value rises to $1100, you would take some profits off the table by selling a portion of your holdings. You may sell enough so that your original investment is back at your desired percentage

(50% now) or more (25% now). Then, you would invest that money in another sector or asset class to regain the balance and diversification of your original portfolio.

If the price of a stock begins to skyrocket, don't invest more money, because when it falls back down, you'll be risking a good deal of your money. If you're unable to resist the temptation and you feel it will only continue rising indefinitely, then consider selling half of your holdings now and wait until after it reaches its peak (so that you aren't tempted to sell more) before selling the rest.

An exception to this rule is if you're trading with a Stop Loss. This is when you sell if the stock falls to a certain price and then wait for the stock to rebound before buying back in at a lower price. That way, no matter what happens, you're not losing any money on that trade.

Don't forget, rebalancing is also applicable to investing in other asset classes besides stocks such as real estate or commodities.

What should I do about taxes?

As an individual investor, it's highly likely you'll be keeping all your investments within one brokerage account (and the same tax-advantaged retirement account). This means that you will be responsible for calculating taxes on those investments. It's important to try to keep all of your investments in one tax-advantaged retirement account, and to keep track of any dividends or short-term capital gains so you can adjust your annual tax return accordingly. What this means is that if you have a mutual fund for your 401K plan, buy stock in the company with cash in your taxable account (or a portion of the 401K), and then sell it after it rises in value—you'll end up paying both short-term and long-term capital gains taxes on that money. Using the same example, you could have bought the same mutual fund with a different broker for your Roth 401K, and then after it rose in value and you had a gain, you could have moved that money into your Roth IRA without paying any taxes.

Having a proper portfolio management can help you to stay cold and increase your chance to make more profit from investments with less risk than not doing anything at all. I will introduce some strategies for investors who are looking for ways to improve their portfolio management skills and overcome emotional trading problem.

As everyone knows, don't be emotional is very important in managing your investment. The market is always changing and sometimes it can move up or move down in a short period of time. If you are trapped by fear, greed or panic, then you have no chance to make more profit but instead you will lose money although you have good investments.

Therefore, we should learn how to control our emotion before trading for any investment. Otherwise it's not easy to make profit even if we have good knowledge about investment and trading techniques.

Few people know that traders can manage the emotions during investing process by using a proper method called "investing psychology". In addition, there are some strategies which can be used to overcome the emotional trading problem.

According to Stock Charts, they mentioned four steps for you. The first one is to set your financial goals and consider how much money you would like to put into the investments. After that, consider your tolerance for risk and determine what kind of investment would be appropriate for you based on your risk tolerance level. (Bear and bull market may cause higher volatility in investment but it doesn't mean that high volatility means higher risk).

Thirdly, decide how long you want to keep the investments and determine what you would do if the market were to decline over a longer period of time from your purchase date. And lastly, establish your investment risk exposure in percentage terms, which will require you to take into account your age and target retirement date.

CONCLUSION

And so we reach this juncture, where it is customarily thought that most readers of this genre would be chomping at the bit, to be let loose on the stock market. I advise caution in this case, and if you have been following closely, you would also have arrived at the same conclusions as myself.

The market is precisely that – a market. There is no emotion, no attachment to it. There is nothing romantic about it, nor is it particularly exciting. The great issue for most is that many tend to mix the stock market up with money, or more precisely, money which they hope to own.

Please step away from that pedestal, and turn your thoughts away from that.

The more you are able to stay dispassionate and relatively cool with regards to the workings and machinations of the stock market or any market of assets, the better it would be for your overall investing endeavor.

To me, the correct application of this book for the seasoned journeyman or for the beginner would be always to go back to the basics. Get a good grasp of the kind of market that you are dealing with. For example, if you should decide that you would like to confine your hunt to just the S&P 500 index stocks, then study those stocks and come to understand the index's movement like you would your own body. This of course, does not happen overnight, and it would require daily conscientious effort in order to work towards it.

With the clarity of targets, the next step would be to formulate your hunting strategy or hunting system. This is where loads of people would be gunning for the easy way out, seduced by this or that readymade system sold by glib salespeople who promise the rolling in of riches with the investment of just an hour a day.

Nothing worthwhile is ever for free. Just think of the duck floating serenely on the surface of the lake, when it is actually paddling constantly to keep afloat beneath the waters. So too should this be a harbinger for how the construction of your personal system be like.

You may run into dead ends, and may even start tearing your hair out from their roots in frustration. That is normal. What matters most at this point would be the tenacious continuation of the search to create your own workable system. I can only say to you – Do Not Give Up. You will be able to find that system eventually, and when you trust it and start seeing the consistent profits from it, that would make all the prior frustrations very worth their while. Your portfolio is unique to you – it serves as a history of the choices you make to achieve your financial goals, and as such it needs to be tuned to your needs. Do not start investing without a plan and make sure you know what you are trying to secure in your investments.

List everything that you wish to accomplish with investments and determine what type of investment strategy best suits that purpose. You will find that you need secure investments and will have the opportunity to make riskier investments as well. Use this opportunity to experiment and to find what opportunities best suit you. I strongly recommended a 529 college savings plan if you have children, but this option might not be the strongest for yourself. Do your research and start to learn how many hours you can dedicate to investing each week. The questions you answer in your financial plan will determine the risk of your investments and their positioning in your portfolio.

Expectations are what identifies success. Millionaires expect to generate income, and more than that, they anticipate their money to make for them. They make choices that are targeted at the objective of turning their cash into more cash, be it from a new financial investment, a new service, or perhaps an innovative enterprise. These action-based choices do not originate from nowhere. Instead, they are the item of vigorous idea procedures that helped turn them into the successful people that they are. Millionaires don't believe negatively and certainly don't see themselves in a negative light. They don't see money as a bad thing but rather see poverty as a bad thing.

Developing a millionaire frame of mind won't happen overnight. It may take years of work to reverse a few of the negative idea patterns, decide every day to provide your best self and live an action-oriented lifestyle.

It is my sincerest wish that you would be able to generate consistent returns from the stock market, and who knows, perhaps one day you would be able to quit your day job and enjoy life solely off the profits from the stock market.

Never give up.

.